FIRE ISLAND AND THEIR SISTER

FÉLIX GARMENDÍA

PEARLSONG PRESS
NASHVILLE, TN

Pearlsong Press
P.O. Box 58065 | Nashville, TN 37205
www.pearlsong.com | www.pearlsongpress.com

Trade paperback ISBN: 978-1-59719-101-2
Ebook ISBN: 978-1-59719-102-9

Photo credits: Author photo by Alexandra Wang. Cover sea glass photo by Cebas1 | Dreamstime. All other photos by Clay Giffin.

The poem "The Book of Fire Island" was first published in *Poems of Reckoning and Hope* (Pearlsong Press, 2022), and is included here with permission.

ALSO BY FÉLIX GARMENDÍA
Flying on Invisible Wings | Poems of Reckoning and Hope

Library of Congress Cataloging-in-Publication Data

Names: Garmendía, Félix, 1961- author.
Title: Fire island and their sister / Félix Garmendía.
Description: Nashville, TN : Pearlsong Press, [2023] | Summary: "In his third book of poetry, Félix Garmendía celebrates the popular LGBTQ+ vacation destinations of Fire Island and commemorates Titania, a trans woman of Manhattan"— Provided by publisher.
Identifiers: LCCN 2022061778 (print) | LCCN 2022061779 (ebook) | ISBN 9781597191012 (trade paperback) | ISBN 9781597191029 (ebook)
Subjects: LCSH: Fire Island (N.Y. : Island)--Poetry. | LCGFT: Poetry. | Gay poetry. | Transgender poetry.
Classification: LCC PS3607.A755 F57 2023 (print) | LCC PS3607.A755 (ebook) | DDC 811/.6—dc23/eng/20230113
LC record available at https://lccn.loc.gov/2022061778
LC ebook record available at https://lccn.loc.gov/2022061779

To My Husband, Denis

Revisiting the sands of Cherry Grove
after 25 years growing together.

INTRODUCTION

Fire Island. Playground to gay folks.

But according to Felix, it turns out that there are three Fire Islands.

The one many of us think of as the summer home of lavish parties, rainbow flags and pageants, come one, come all—Cherry Grove.

The Pines—summer home to younger gay men.

Saltaire, Ocean Beach, Sailors Haven—where families hang out. Except when a few of them high-tail it to Cherry Grove at night, to return with secret smiles on their faces.

There is also a fourth Fire Island—the Fire Island of fauna. Deer, raccoons, cats, dogs, mice, sea birds of many kinds.

Felix writes of all four Fire Islands with humor, gusto and grace. He beckons us, especially but not only those of us who have never been there, to board that ferry.

Then there is Titania.

She is the other side of the coin, a trans woman who lives on the edge of society's "lawful" dictates.

Life for her is closer to the way it used to be fifty years ago, even twenty, for many of the gay men who now flock to Fire Island. At night she slips from shadow to shadow in the Meatpacking district, then celebrates by day in gay bars in the Village. She grows into her identity, finding herself and redefining herself by the rules she derives from her surroundings and from her wishes.

This book presents two related kinds of lives as they strive toward legitimacy.

In the past few years, the rights of gay and trans people have again come under attack by haters. Suddenly the lives led by those on Fire Island and in the Village are in jeopardy once more.

Felix's vivid, amusing but uncompromising portraits, his and their pride in every space and sinew, become ours. Along with him and Titania, we must stand up for them to be more than nostalgia, that they be able to inhabit the world that is, and part of the world to be.

F. GHAURI
Editor

Fire Island.

The music is electric, the sky wears the blue of a promise, rainbows fly everywhere, the beach, sprinkled with beach glass and content people, breathes freedom. I'm surrounded by my kind in a community with a history of queer color.

Men hold hands without fear of ridicule. Here, it doesn't matter anymore that at some point in my past I tried too hard to explain myself when I was still reading my map to manhood. People are polite. Saying hello on the boardwalks is not uncommon.

I'm guaranteed room to grow my soul in Cherry Grove. I feel more than tolerance: encouragement for uniqueness. A shared celebration.

Cherry Grove embraces my needed healing. Fire Island is more than a second home. It's an affirmation of my truest self.

Félix Sarmendía

Sunday, September 4, 2022, 9:13 pm

My husband, Félix Garmendía, IS a POET and now I KNOW IT!

Felix's magical journey through Cherry Grove is joyful and comforting. I first stepped onto Fire Island about 50 years ago and thought I was on another planet. Cherry Grove, Fire Island is a miracle place and Felix knows it!

Barefoot disco dancing in a bathing suit was one of my favorite joyous activities in Cherry Grove.

There is no traffic because there are NO cars. There are no cars because there are NO roads—only wooden boardwalks.

Running into baby deer on the boardwalk was always a wonderful surprise for Felix and me.

DENIS BEALE

CONTENTS

GLOSSARY

Bear—large and or tall man with body hair, usually older than 30.

Cub—much younger bear (younger than 25).

Cherry Grove—section of Fire Island known for eclectic parties and events; embraces a wide demographic of gay people of all sexual orientations, appearances and ages; welcoming to hetero people as well.

Daddy—protective older man (older than 30).

Faun—young, hairless, often inexperienced male.

Leather man—characterized by a fetish for leather gear, a sense of hierarchy and a fraternal code of protocol and behavior; often sexually involved in BDSM (bondage/discipline, dominance/submission, sadism/masochism).

Master—in a sexual relationship, someone who maintains control and often orders the participant or participants about.

The Meat Rack, a.k.a. The Rack—stretch of sand walk between Cherry Grove and The Pines, renowned for easy accessibility of sexual encounters.

Otter—younger bear (younger than 30).

The Pines—section of Fire Island inhabited by younger gay men (mostly under 50).

Poppers—amyl nitrite drug used to induce a pleasant or euphoric sensation; often accompanies dancing and or sexual activity.

Slave—in a sexual relationship, someone who takes orders from a master and obeys.

Twink—homosexual male with "attractive" boyish qualities: smooth, often hairless skin, slim. Usually younger than 30.

FIRE ISLAND

The Book of Fire Island

Jesus dies
every year
on the clock.
It's been
32 minutes since
the
most recent
death.
He goes into
seclusion
for a long
weekend
starting Friday,
ending Sunday.
I hear
apocryphal books
tell the real story.
Where is Jesus
for 3 days?
The word is clear,
he escapes
to Fire Island
with his best
friend,
Mary Magdalene.
She pays for the
gas,
they take
the

Long Island
Expressway.
She wants
to visit the nude
beach and admire
bodies.
Her bronze
middle-eastern
skin
glows under the
Cherry Grove sun,
where she basks
while
Jesus
downs mojitos
at
the Ice Palace
bar.
Mary Magdalene
will meet him
there
before dinner
but after lunch.
Jesus chats
away
with the locals,
making jokes,
getting tipsy
watching
a conga line
forming at the disco.
He's cool with

           FIRE ISLAND AND THEIR SISTER

two men kissing.
And two proud lesbians
with
their adopted child.

Mary Magdalene shows
up
wearing
a Hawaiian
sarong
and
they dance
till the sun
slides down.

Minutes before
Sunday,
they're
both back
in town.
Golgotha
is wondering
if he'll rise.
Jesus
orders the
earthquake,
the Roman guards
notice
the stone moving.

When Mary Magdalene
looks at Jesus's feet,

she wonders:
How in heaven's name
will he explain
the rainbow
sandals?

Drag Kings

Faces with no makeup.
Mustaches, beards, sideburns, fedoras,
but no big wigs or gowns.
The less known of their kind.
They use uniforms,
and become
cops,
doctors,
Wall Street robots,
regular Joes,
rock stars;
we even have our very own Elvis.
I notice them in the invasion.
Some are bartenders.
Fixtures at the dock
welcoming the
ferries from Sayville.
Around town,
their humor
and mischief
clothe them
in sport jackets,
wing tips,
ties
and pants.
These lesbians:
the other side of the record,
an old
Fire Island tradition.

A different song,
a queer voice.

Another drummer.

　　　FIRE ISLAND AND THEIR SISTER

Drag Queen College

The professionals
know how to avoid mishaps,
walking tipsy on stilettos
without falling off the boardwalks.
The younger ones end up snoring on the grass.
The experts
use hemorrhoid cream as a foundation
to erase lines.
The new girls
use a ton of makeup which melts
under the Fire Island sun.
You can tell the amateur ones
by
the walk some can't hide.
One breast falsie bigger than the other.
They haven't mastered high heels.
Cheap eyelashes that fall off.
Breaking nails opening beers.
Stepping on their gowns.
while dancing at the Ice Palace.
Many fail Drag Queen 101.

But that doesn't keep them
from trying.

Cherry Grove Unplugged

Umbrellas and music,
pot smoke,
coolers full of beer
and the coconut smell of suntan lotion.
I kick waves before they foam
under my bare feet.
On my way to nowhere,
I admire the melted glass of ocean.
Aquamarine sheet reaches the horizon.

Cherry Grove and a Blunt

The recipe Martha Stewart won't give you.
A tobacco leaf rolling paper
starts the ritual.
The grinding of the pot
breaks
the pollen crystals.
The fragrance
from the blossom
emerges.
Licking
commences the preparation of
the cylinder
about to be sparked.
Exiting my home on Holly Walk,
blunt and lighter in hand,
I take the first puff
where the Ice Palace's corner
meets the bay's view.
My eyes dilate.
I'm Cheech
looking for a Chong.
Not much fun to smoke alone.

Wow! That cloud looks like Willie Nelson!

Behind the Tide

Beachcombers, mostly locals,
get up early, before the first ferry,
to collect beach glass
while the seashore is free of visitors.
Tumbled by the waves and swirls of sand,
beer bottle fragments give green and brown,
the most common of all.
Everyone looks for the elusive ruby color.
The coveted one.
For my life, I can't imagine where it comes from.
An ocean offering from before my time.
Among specs of frosted glass and garnet sand,
the rare fossilized shark tooth.
Kerosene lamps with coral attached.
Chewed up smoking pipes
tangled up in seaweed.
Polished pebbles,
seashells,
starfish.
Medicine bottles, silverware.
Driftwood
used to decorate gardens
and home name signs.
An undercover meteorite
passes as an Earth rock.

Endangered Leather (Rant)

Most have never been to a dungeon
but they know when Gucci has a sale.
Their idea of leather
sprouts from the concept of
what looks good.
Indifferent to tradition,
they shave chests and legs
—claiming it shows muscle tone—
pay thousands for Louis Vuitton
fake leather.
Wax eyebrows
to shape them like Jennifer Lopez's
shaved underarms.
They don't understand the bandanna code
or care for the appropriate use of
left and right
to indicate
top or bottom.
White sneakers with leather shorts.
And Cartier chains.
When faced with a sling,
they lie down backwards.
Combine polo shirts with their slave chokers,
designer jeans instead of
jockstraps under chaps.
Not a shadow of the original.
When leather men were
rugged.
natural,

unshaven.

Bears are endangered.

   FIRE ISLAND AND THEIR SISTER

Between the Cracks

A new bear in town.
Ralph Lauren floral shirt,
linen trousers,
Italian espadrilles.
Vintage fedora
with a pheasant feather.
His demeanor,
calm and collected.
His nails, manicured.
Voice wise,
a melodic Bostonian accent
with an oboe tone.
He must know Provincetown.
Looking into his eyes,
I see adventure.
Maybe it's just because
he reminds me of Sean Connery.
Smilewise,
ample like Cheshire Cat.
Should I offer a drink,
or to dance?
He's with a young woman.
She seems like a sister.
Biological or fruit fly?
It's tea dance time.
Cherry Grove has
no shortage of fish.

He's adorable but my gaydar

didn't move.
This one falls between the cracks.

Fire Island Fossil (Rant)

Many tides away,
in those days,
people used to talk.
Today, they stare at their phones.
A drag show used to spice up the afternoon,
a stroll around town to keep up
with the locals.
The ubiquitous stop at the Ice Palace,
getting tipsy,
dancing,
going home for a shower
and dinner at a local restaurant.
Fire Island nap:
it killed the time between supper and
dusk.

Next stop,
Meat Rack
till the morning sun would hurt my
eyes.

Harmony

Smoke unveils the suspended scent
of salt.
The occasional cigar from a leather man.
Drag queen perfume.
The sky is
bleeding red, pink and orange.
Neon in bars.
Lights in gardens,
buildings remind me of Burano.
The sky
ignites
as the sun sinks into the bay.
Bats flutter in circles over the milkweed fields.
And music from the Ice Palace
blasts
queer anthems.
"I will Survive"
packs the dance floor.
"MacArthur Park"
(with its mysterious cake under the rain).
"We Are Family"
(fact).

The distant crashing of waves.

A Day Well Spent

Dominick dressed as a pope
blessing houses,
old tradition in The Grove.
Drag queens, the "Grovettes,"
usually beat the Suffolk
police, "Copettes,"
in volleyball,
right across from our home.
We have front row seats.
After savoring victory
I stop by
the Cherry Grove
Community House and Theater
to check out what they are staging.
Vanilla shake from Linda's,
a stroll through the supermarket
to enjoy the a/c and escape the sun
while I finish my beverage.
Floyd's becomes
my lunch spot.
Bacon and egg on a roll
with grape soda.
About time for "Cherry's Bar"
to watch the ferries come in
and play bingo
with the drag queen calling
the numbers.

"B-9,"

Félix Garmendía

she screeches
with a smirk.

HOLLYWOOD SLUSH

If naked,
be ready to get sand up all
your crevices.
Your eyes sting.
Your hair gets
caked with a mixture of
seaweed, sand slush, broken shells—
like singing in the rain,
it just doesn't work
in the real world.
Deborah Kerr and Burt Lancaster
immortalized the myth
rolling with the waves.
They must still be spitting sand
and getting it out of their butts
for eternity.
A drink has its name
maybe because you
need to be drunk to attempt it.

Sandy waves? Or a comfy bed
with clean sheets?

Where the Boys Are (Groove in the Grove)

I want an astronaut suit
to avoid steroid allergies.
We celebrate age, icons of gay rights,
people like you
and the neighbor living down the block.
Cookie cutter Ken dolls,
during summer migration,
tend to flock to The Pines.
At night,
in the darkness of the Meat Rack,
what's available
becomes everyone's
fruit to grab.

"Where are you staying,
Cherry Grove or The Pines?"

Fire Island in a Towel, If That

Drag
queens leave
feather trails
on the hot
boardwalks of
Cherry Grove.

The
Ice Palace Disco
dances to memories,
charged
'80s anthems.

The house named,
appropriately,
"YMCA."
Another one with
two golden
griffins.
The fisherman's
cottage
with
wrought iron
gates
and
candlelit
entrance path.

The
Belvedere
Guest House.
Enough said.

Shooting stars,
constellations,
and the
occasional thunderstorm
over
the ocean's
horizon.

I wonder
if the Meat Rack
fauns
remember
my name.

          FIRE ISLAND AND THEIR SISTER

THE MEAT RACK

Men
in search
of men.
Labyrinth
between
Cherry Grove
and
The Pines.
Oasis
of
cravings.
Men of
all shapes
and ages
find
there's more than
one
for everyone.
Twink, daddy;
Slave, master.
Bear, cub.
The otters
hang around.
Group games,
poppers,
pot smoke.
The scent
of booze

in some kisses
day and night.

24/7
on
summer days.

     FIRE ISLAND AND THEIR SISTER

HUNT'S HAPPY PLACE

One summer afternoon,
Hunt calls the only agent in town.
Mrs. Cantrell answers the phone,
"Jesus Takes the Wheel Travel Agency,
how can I help you?"
"Like to go to Cherry Grove,
hear it has a nice beach.
Stay for a weekend
in a place way different than these here Tennessee
hills."

Hunt
packs jeans, boots,
some booze for the trip,
Bible, gun,
three shirts,
looks forward to
South Carolina coast.

Geez, he thinks
as the Greyhound bus
picks its way through traffic.
This sure is taking longer
than I thought.

Hunt lands in town,
traffic-awed,
somehow corrals a cab to Sayville
and follows the advice

of two guys to the ferry.
The summer sun
glints off his shirt snaps.
Someone in the crowd
sings "YMCA."
Hunt's glad to hear
them praising it.
Several people say hello.

"Could be drag,"
says Vaselynn Cummings,
Cherry Grove's homecoming queen,
as he observes Hunt.
"Then again—"

On his way to the Ice Palace Hotel,
Hunt admires:
rainbow flags,
people
holding hands,
the boardwalks—

During the show,
and a few drinks,
people laugh at the performer;
he does too.

Nice old place, this Cherry Grove.
But why did they call those ladies
"drag?"

And why did the travel lady
not say anything
about all the happy
guys?

Secrets That Dare Not Smile

Ocean Beach: 79 residents,
white bread and lettuce sandwich
with a side of boredom
and one thin
road
connecting them
to The Grove.
Nothing
from other communities
except the snoring
of the stars.
From Point O' Woods
to Kismet,
some
take water taxis to

Cherry Grove
for Drag Queen Bingo,
the bars,
and, yes, the Meat Rack.
When asked,
they always claim to be lost.
Wasted and full of joy,
they sneak back to
Davis Park,
Water Island,
Sailors Haven,
Saltaire.
And sleep the night.

Some wake with a smile.

In the Shadows

No stars or moon,
but his eyes
glow like a full moon by the
seashore at night.
He walks pale, like sun-bleached
driftwood.
Until
the boardwalks are deserted,
he roams the paths,
waits for the next man.
Tall, skin scented with night and sea,
cat of dark demeanor.
It's 3 am,
time to take flight.
He spots
his life source
tied up
on his knees.
Opens wide his wings and
swallows his catch in an embrace
while his prey moans.

Later he returns to his cauldron
and circles the lamp post
over the milkweed patch.
Licks his lips,
still savoring.

Time for another.

Fire Island Water Taxi

Invading (My Alter Egos)

I
The Vegas girl wore:
silver sequined gown,
emerald green ostrich feathered headdress,
1950s crocodile high heels,
blue wig.
Pearl earrings,
art deco filigree diamond pendant.
Blue eye shadow,
fake eyelashes
emphasized with an eyebrow pencil,
natural mole next to
crimson glossy lips.
She got drunk
and missed the ferry back to The Grove,
wobbled along the Meat Rack,
getting her headdress tangled up in low branches,

and tottering in heels on sand.

II
Self portrait
with crucified hummingbird necklace
hanging from a choker of thorns:
Frida
carried a stuffed monkey,
leather sandals and a sign that read,
"I hate Diego!"
She

mingled with
Mona Lisa,
frame and all,
and
Liza Minnelli.

In another life,
Bette Midler.

MEAT

You'd think we are vampires
cruising the night in the Meat Rack.
After all the bars close
a crescent moon fails to dissipate the darkness
after midnight,
way after.
Nobody wears watches in the dark.
Or talks;
phones go on vibrate.
No flashlights.
And from Cherry Grove to The Pines,
only the crashing of waves pierces the silence
among occasional moans.
Willing men have been swapping pleasures
in the wooded area
for the longest time.
There are
naked men leaning against trees.
The ones on their knees
looking up,
waiting for a top.
The occasional slave
willingly
chained up to a low branch
being shared with all
by his master.
Some watch.
I grow tentacles
and in groups,

taste and touch as many men as I can.
No time to waste.

From the east,
sun rays start to crack the tinted
glass of the night.

Who Gets the Crown?

Drag queens invade The Pines.
Monarchs take over Cherry Grove
on their way to Mexico
during their aristocratic migration.
They stop to feed on milkweed.
Queen Elizabeth, across the pond,
lives
oblivious to the pleasures of lesser lineage.
She prefers crumpets and biscuits
while wearing tiaras.
Monarch butterflies, nature's royalty,
mingle well with the Fire Island queens.

Night Waking

The horizon ignites; thunderstorms crawl over the
ocean.
Constellations studded with eyes of fire
and planets extend their arms.
The waves rise and fall.
The salt water mists,
clouds go to sleep.

Green eyes awake and on fire
meet the island of fire.

Rusted Car Talk

What year is it?
It's 2022.
Remember the time the S&M top
handcuffed his boy to your bumper?
Yes, I do.
Then the dumb ass lost the key cruising the Meat
Rack!
And when he came back, Boy Gregg was gone.
I have a feeling those two had a huge kerfuffle!
I remember your story about the guy who
hid his clothing on your seat.
Yes, he wanted to cruise the Meat Rack naked.
And when he came back,
a brown recluse in his pants
stung him.
I still recall the "Macarena" dance
when the spider said hello to his left sack.
Do you remember the porn actors from that flick?
Yes, the sequel of "Fire Island Wet Dreams."
It rained all day.
They had to move the shooting to
the Belvedere Guest House.
They all waited under the trees for an hour
until they gave up and left when their leather got
drenched!
They smelled like wet dogs.
The things we've seen—
Shhhh.
Here comes Bruce and his boy.

The ones who like to take pictures naked near you?
Yes, those two.

I don't complain.
We were abandoned
but we'll never be alone.

Stormy Night

I summon darkness to explode in lightning bolts.
Over the horizon,
rumbling in the distance,
electric avalanche of brightness over the ocean.
It's been four years since my last visit to Fire Island.
I miss the rainpour hitting the wooden roof.
The fragrance of salt and rain
caught in angry winds.
Bolts slashing the shadows
causing day to show up for seconds
only to die with one blink—
wet boardwalks getting softer under my feet.

In bed, covered in thick blankets,
watching the curtains
pushed by the gale
that enters the bedroom:
ghosts looking for shelter from the storm.
I want to defy nature, enjoying what most fear:
when the night roars like a hungry beast.
Protection from the raindrops
in my den
as the stormy evening
washes away footprints and sand
from deserted boardwalks.

The Ruby

Red: fresh blood,
pear cut,
custom made gold nipple ring,
glistened many summers
under the Fire Island sun,
then sported shirtless at leather bars.
Now reincarnated
as a left eyebrow piercing,
most of the time hidden by glasses
but still at times,
an accessorized wink

in photos.

SAND AND SNOW

The ocean's music slows down;
a sheet of steel faces the muted sunlight.
Snowflakes.
Wildlife paw prints decorate them.
The bay freezes.
Ice chunks float on thick waters.
Crowds are gone, a few residents remain.
Cherry Grove hibernates.
The island's fire takes an extended nap.
A few ferries navigate the bay;
occasional deer feed on evergreens.
A lone seal at the seashore basks in the morning sun.
Nights, illuminated by frozen starlight.
Snow crystals compete with the sparkle of garnet
    sand
left behind by revolving tides.

Where My Books* Hang Out

A pharmacy in Washington Heights:
Condoms, KY lube.
And a display of funny looking socks.
They depict hamburgers, tacos and beer,
green aliens in spaceships,
Frida Kahlo with her monkeys
and
New York City's Miss Liberty.

Grove Market, Cherry Grove:
Behind the cash register.
Where cigarettes,
batteries,
lighters
and
rolling paper
keep them company.

Rainbows & Dreams,
also in Cherry Grove:
"The Oral Sex Game,"
"Bondage Seductions,"
"My Journey to Love"
stand next to
"My Penis."
Drag attire,
sex toys,
poppers,
and rainbows

          FIRE ISLAND AND THEIR SISTER

are
for sale,
along with
dreams.

Time for you, The Pines?

Flying On Invisible Wings (Pearlsong Press), *Poems of Reckoning and Hope* (Pearlsong Press).

After the Last Ferry

I
Late arrival, misplaced ferry schedule.

Some lucky ones
hook up with a local,
score a place to spend the night.
Others walk in circles.
Some sleep on the beach.
Some men go to
the forested playground in the Meat Rack.
The hours age faster.

II
Sunglasses,
sand on crotch,
mosquito bites,
chafed knees,
messed up hair,
eye bags
that smile
as they grab the first ferry next morning.

You can tell.

Angles

Some men instinctively find
where the lamp's switch is.
They genuinely enjoy
pulling the cord.
Some know
where to mold the clay
and point
a finger
on the vessel.

The willing develop
a sexual Esperanto.

On Fire Island I knew
the geometry of
male pleasure.
Like a maestro
I taught tenors
how to reach
the high notes.

ELROY FINDS HUNT

Elroy boards the ferry to Cherry Grove.
Snap shirt, dungarees, cowboy hat and boots.
Cherry Grove Inn,
where at 87 degrees, Elroy insists on wearing his
cowboy hat and boots. They are attached to him
like ostrich feather headdresses to Cher and drag
    queens.
Elroy ventures into town.
Drag queens,
leather men,
lesbians, gays, trans folks, bisexuals, the curious—
Elroy stands among them like a vision escaped from
    "Gunsmoke."
Nobody bats an eye.
Not even the queen with a fake eyelash stuck to her
    contact lens.
He stops by the nearest bar,
needing a few shots to cope.
"Straight Christian Brothers Brandy please, keep
    'em coming.
I'm waitin' for the winged monkeys to come and
    snatch me away,"
he giggles, and hears the bartender call him by
    name.
Astonished, Elroy looks up.
"Elroy! A small stinkin' world, my man.
What you doin' so far away from home?
How do you like New York?"
"I don't. I hate it.

Those damn Yankees live like termites in towers.
The rats in the subway have their own damn zip
    code!"
"Elroy, it ain't that bad.
Been here for a while by now.
Make a living in paradise.
This is a different world, my man.
Here, we relax and watch the sunset."
"Doesn't that get old after a while?"
"Not any more than back home."
"What do you mean?"
Hunt laughs.
"Does it really matter?
Not here.
Cheers, this one is on me."
All through that night
and the rest
and—the rest,
Elroy starts to wonder.
As he sees the queens and kings
and all the other folk, queer and other,
getting drunk, running around and laughing,
having such a damn good time—
not to mention Hunt—
and not caring about what anyone is
or where they're from,
or who their pappies were
or weren't—
just how much, he keeps wondering,
does it really matter?

Félix Garmendía

TITANIA

About Titania

Titania, the legendary queen, often shows herself on the Lower East Side of Manhattan. Titania is very much like my friend Philippe, one of the early casualties of AIDS. He told me personal stories which I've included in sections of Titania's life.

In Titania I see a display of colors that some of us are afraid to connect with. Her resilience becomes a map to a destination that forces her to make decisions in survival mode. Titania is bright, independent, compassionate, strong, militant about her convictions and a friend to many. She could be any member of your immediate family or that woman that you've been saying hello to for years and about whose daily challenges you have no clue.

Titania finds ways to validate herself regardless of the circumstances surrounding her reality. That strength of wanting to live connects her to us.

Félix Garmendía
August 23, 2022

I am honored that Felix has asked me to write an introduction to the poetry he has so eloquently written about an all-too-familiar character we all knew in the New York City of the 1980s and '90s, Titania.

I actually knew Marsha Johnson, Sylvia Rivera, "Ivan the Terrible" and so many others from my years managing the door at Club Edelweiss both on 29th Street and after it relocated to 11th Avenue. And as a trans woman of that era I can attest that he has truly captured not just the reality of the times but the intimate feelings of the characters he is writing about.

Superb job—thank you, Felix.

Robyn Murray

By the third poem, I had fallen in love with Titania.

She is often the other side of the coin from Fire Island: living and expressing her sexuality at night, in the shadows, as society seemingly permits.

As she finds herself and carves out her identity, we divine a lusty, proud, sometimes fearful, always edgy trans woman who enjoys her work at times, knows how to celebrate and have fun, and always seems to be one step ahead of the police or bad johns.

Bilingual, she expresses herself with gusto and with thoroughness in two languages. And she continues to love and honor her mom, Milagros, who gives her Francisco—her former male identity—whom she then turns into Titania, her newer name and life.

Felix writes her with love, sorrow and a
thoroughly intuitive and insightful understanding.
Thank you, Felix.

F. GHAURI
Editor

Titania: The Beginning

I
Titania, Colombian on her mother's side, doesn't
    talk
about dad: dark bar, drunk stranger:
a night of $20 hookups.

"Francisco Torres" carries her mother's last name.
Watches Hollywood movies.
Dreams of being Grace Kelly.
Wants his prince to come.

II
Francisco-Titania looks in the garbage for
    magazines, dreams of wearing Chanel.
She becomes a queen.
The Christopher Street piers play home to her.
The fogs bring ship sounds, hosts of sailors.
Once it brought her mother.

At least one will play.
Titania
lifts her lamp and more
beside what is golden.

A Splash of Evangeline

She wears her olive skin
wet still from showering before work.
Midnight:
Titania starts with blue eyeshadow. Blood rose lips.
A splash of Evangeline inherited from mom.
The shy light in the room carves her curves
in reflections improved by a Cuba Libre mix of rum
     and coke.
Stockings ripped by runs of many nights giving in
     the back of johns' cars.
Oversized T-shirt, no bra.
Panties help her hide "Francisco."
Some clients know Francisco very well and like it.
     Others pretend it doesn't exist.
Titania introduces Francisco when she knows it will
     be embraced, maybe even kissed.
"Sensible shoes tonight, in case I have to bolt from
     the police," she says to the mirror.
Covers her moustache shadow with off color base
     she stole from the pharmacy on 14th street.
Transformed, she kisses the mirror.
Turns off the lights.

Her audience is waiting.
The entire Meatpacking District* is her stage.

The show must go on.

*Meatpacking District—area of Manhattan, now
upscale, in which were located a number of sex clubs
and bars in the 1980s.

TITANIA'S 23RD BIRTHDAY

Jo calls the three girls:
Altagracia, Carmen, Ana,
sisters of the night. To Titania:
"Girl, come over, I'm bored. Got some great ganja."
The girls giggle.
The A train to Inwood.
Her steps know the street.

2 C.
Girls quiet down
from being happy on Mad Dog.
Jo turns off the lights.
Titania can't believe her eyes.
"SURPRISE!" yells, balloons, rainbow glitter
    birthday sign.
"Happy Birthday to you, *cumpleaños feliz!*"
Cake from Gideon's bakery,
bagels,
apple strudel,
black-and-whites for after the joint.

Titania calls, "Best time
I had standing up. Evah."

She passes the joint and sips her Mad Dog.

Titania's Dream

Titania crashes on Josefa's couch
a subway ride away,
makeup and clothes still on.

She and Josefa protect each other from dangerous
    johns
who vanish now, when they share a joint.

In sleep, she visits
Alphabet City, crafting mandalas with pebbles,
in Tompkins Square Park: Needle Park.
She reinvents the child, childhood,
draws hopscotch with chalk
in her yellow dress
as her hair teases the wind.

For a few hours,
she forgets Francisco
completely.

Titania Dreams Milagros

Baby dresses in pastel colors,
matching crochet socks,
flower diadems, ribbons,
teaching her to dance salsa and merengue
as mom's laughter competes with the chords of
    Willie Colón.
"Stay near me
where I can see you."
Titania buys a doll,
gingham in blue,
red ruby slippers, Toto stuffed animal sold
    separately.
Titania and Milagros, sharing pink cloud cotton
    candy,
following the golden opal dawn,
cobblestone streets of downtown.

Titania's Rosary

Glow of the dark beads including the crucifix.
"Francisco, get ready, we are going to mass at 3."

Rosary in hand,
the more she prays
the lonelier she feels.
But the fear:
a panic of ending it all in worms and dirt.
"It's all about faith," echoes in her ears.
"There has to be more than this."
Titania thinks God.
Makes the sign of the cross.
Clutches in her hand the crucifix.
Apostles' Creed.
"I believe in God the Father almighty,
maker of heaven and earth… "
A mantra learned from mom.
Just in case…

Titania's Fix

Crystal meth from one of the girls moonlighting to
    spread stars
under the abandoned elevated rail.
Needle in her vein,
constellation of punctures in her arm,
colors and scattered memories,
she crossbows the phoenix.
Titania leans against a graffitied wall.
Symphonic voices.
The rush passes, her cat pupils dilate.
Following the tracks of a forgotten rail,
she emerges on her usual corner.
Meatpacking district.

Another working night.

TITANIA AND LA LUPE

Mom's old records:
"La Lupe."
"Electric woman, strong voiced Cubana."
Latin soul, boleros, guarachas—
Ballads on rainy days having her Cuba Libres in
    Alphabet City.
La Lupe's salsa with Francisco, Titania's long-ago
    boy name.
"She sings pain in a way nobody else can, believing
    in feverish love that consumes itself."

Mom's voice translates.

Meth

In the turmoil of a dream
images swirl into separate lines, now dragged down.
The past drains into lava
as Titania sweats acid that corrodes,
memories that hurt like melted rock on awakened
    skin:
the time she ran from a violent john,
Mom's overdose,
Francisco bullied in high school, everywhere.

A shower of nails on her soul
that gasps for air.

Titania at Christmas

Three blocks exploding with lights and colors:
skaters sliding, birds flying within an inch of the
    ground.
Kneels slightly, makes the sign of the cross close to
    St. Patrick's.
Atlas upholds the heavens,
spirals.
At the end of a hall of light,
the king tree towers.

Titania remembers
a newly opened crayon box.
Titania remembers—
Mom singing to José Feliciano's ¡*"Feliz Navidad"!*
Eating *pasteles,* roast pork, *arroz con gandules* at the
    food kitchen
in Alphabet City.
"The Peanuts Christmas Special" on TV.
The aluminum tree reflecting blue, red, green and
    yellow
that Christmas when Francisco got the Chatty
    Cathy doll
Mom found on her way home from work.

"Merry Christmas to me."
Titania walks alone down the snow-covered streets
near Rockefeller Center.

Titania Does Hamilton

3 pm:
Titania shares a few blunts with Jo in Inwood
before hitting the streets.
She takes the A train,
dozes off for a few stops,
in a panic, exits the train when woken up by the
      loudspeaker:
"145th Street."
"*Carajo, coño,* where the fuck am I?
What a rat hole of a station, it smells like *mierda.*"

The neighborhood hot *papis*
don't even notice her.
Bodegas, barber shops, Iglesia de Dios Pentecostal—
Music escaping cars,
children on sidewalks
still wearing school uniforms.
Bird murals by a local artist
squint at Titania from above, like silent gods.
She walks the blunts off,
stops by KFC to kill her blunt-made munchies.

Carajo, the subway is where?

Titania Goes to Church

Sunday afternoon, St. Veronica's Church on
    Christopher Street.
Grey skies and rain invite her in.
Remembers going with mom as a kid, wearing her
    best T-shirt and her
school shoes.
Titania kneels down, genuflects and crosses herself,
just like mom used to
do.
Still scared from last night's close call, the john that
    almost beat her,
she gives thanks to a god that
forgot her long ago.
The congregation smells the night on her.
Titania gets tapped on the shoulder.
Older man: "Did you confess? They are about to
    give the Eucharist."
"I have nothing to confess," she replies.

As she leaves, denied by the priest,
she remembers now
why she did not return.

Titania in Front of Cartier's (A Mother's Day Poem)

Titania always wanted blue eyes
like Elizabeth Taylor's.
These sapphires, mom's favorite,
look just like the ones johns give to wives
out of guilt
or to keep them quiet.
Titania becomes Julia Roberts
opening her present from Richard Gere,
the mechanics
of the box
unfamiliar—
startles her with a string of stars.

Titania smiles, as her mom
once did—
eyes closed.

Titania's Pride

She goes straight to her closet.
Chooses her cotton yellow dress.
The one that reminds her of an old childhood
    dream.
Puts makeup on.
Steps out.
Takes the subway to Christopher Street.
It's the end of June.
She's there to catch the end of the Pride Parade.
Titania waits in the crowd
with a bag of confetti.
Her hair flowing freely in the wind,
Titania waits for the
"Survivors of Stonewall"
convertible car
presenting the last of the heroes
with a blasting rendition
of "We Are the Champions" by
Freddie Mercury and Queen.
She joins the end of the parade.
Waving and shaking hands with marchers,
she walks to the final
destination.
Vendors sell rainbows and
drag queens entertain,
lip synching to
the tune of Katy Perry's
"Fireworks"
in a medley

following
"I am what I am"
and Lady Gaga's
"Born This Way."

Titania dances.
Free.

   FIRE ISLAND AND THEIR SISTER

Cherry Lips

Bears roam Weehawken street
at Sunday's
beer blast.
Titania stops by
to say hello
and get a drink or two
at Badlands.
They
know her by now.
She sits under
a tree to burn a blunt
and lace
it with her lager.
It's a crisp blue sky
Sunday in July.
The boys are proudly shirtless:
harnesses,
pierced nipples,
navel, septum, eyebrow
piercings,
tattoos
and cruising
are on the brunch
menu.
Hungry men
hunting.

Entranced by
the crowds

and the
balmy weather.
Titania sits
and watches
the daddy
caressing his young man.
The master
with his smiling slave.
The bear playing
with a cub,
the admiring otters.
She remembers
her Sundays
as a kid.
Mom's pink
plastic rosary,
her mantilla,
missal,
wearing
her best shoes, skirt
and blouse.
For him,
white shirt,
long blue pants,
black and white
saddle shoes.
Francisco
sits through
mass.
Not knowing the
right words to answer

          FIRE ISLAND AND THEIR SISTER

or the time to kneel,
he daydreams
about the cherry Italian ice
mom buys him every Sunday
on their way back
to their apartment in Alphabet City.
He loves how
it turns his lips red.

Like mom's
on her way to work.

Goodbye to Marsha*

Two days after 4th of July 1992,
shortly after Pride parade,
"With Liberty and Justice For All,"
the sky still hurting from fireworks,
the Mayor of Christopher Street is dead,
Titania hears from the girls.
"They found her floating in the East River.
Wound behind her head."
"Some say she was bullied by a group of thugs,"
    comments Josefa,
"but cops said suicide."
"Bullshit," yells Titania, "she wasn't suicidal."

Titania remembers:
laughter,
the joint they shared,
gossip about the girls and johns,
Marsha and her love of life.

Titania fears for her own.

Marsha Johnson, famous trans activist.

Meatpacking District Titania

She salutes the crowds of the Meatpacking District.
    Some salute her.
Wears her face: cracked porcelain to be restored.
In red and purple with crooked silver heels,
    stockings marked with runs hidden away from
    the police.
Cigarette dangling, Queen Titania parades herself,
    pantyless, at 3 am in and out of the piers,
    preening her hunger.
A quick fix.
She hides whom she calls "Puck" by a new name
    from the seam of her short skirt.
Titania works after hours for many, disappears when
    the day wanders behind the piers.
She returns, regrouping; women arrive one by one
    from being packed by meat,
the district of their midsummer night's dream.
Titania counts her girls, sleeps the day away covered
    with the moss of dollars under her pillow.

Titania Rollerblading in Central Park

Titania pulls out her Walkman.
Listening to *"El Gran Combo,"* she dances on
   wheels with a Latin beat: hips and heart.
Drums blasting in her earphones,
Titania salsas herself into the city forest.
She jumps, beats syncopating.

Titania skates her soul,
the Crab Walk shifts her toes over small hills.
The Iceberg: skating backwards landing on the
   inner sides of the skates. Sliding the edges of
   wheels flying just above the pavement.
The Traveling Toe Pivot, switching her balance from
   the tip of one foot alternating, gliding close to
   the edge of the sidewalk.

The Snake Walk.
Skates downhill
bolting into a pirouette.

Passersby high five her.

Titania On the Road Again

Gentrified midtown neighbor dials 911.
"—prostitute from my window selling drugs."
Titania camouflages
in a dark alley.

"You have the **right** to remain silent. Anything you
    say can and will be used against you in a court of
    law—"
Handcuffed Titania
turns up
empty plastic bag, white powder residue.
Syringe,
elastic band.
No stranger to the routine,
another cop recognizes her from priors.
Titania Torres:
Solicitation, possession, drug paraphernalia.
"On the road again, Titania?"
Titania bows her head.
The first cop explains her rights.
In the paddy wagon downtown,
same song and dance.
Released with another court date she will ignore.

The gentrified neighbor inhales perfect lemon
    ginger tea
as she closes her window.
Too much noise.

Titania Meets Dana

80 Grove Street.
The Monster piano bar.
Sundays, no cover.
Go-go boys,
downstairs disco.
Titania hooks up with beer.

Lower level:
'70s and '80s dance tunes.
Leather queens, fags, trannies, dykes, preppy boys,
    drag queens—Titania jumps in.
Bee Gees' "Stayin' Alive" brings the crowd together.
Titania dances with another trans woman:
Blonde hair, bright eyes,
jeans with high heels, designer type blouse.
"Hi, I'm Dana, and you are?"
"Titania." They scream to each other over the
    music, under the mirror ball.

Outside:
Dana and Titania smoke a cigarette.
Evening falls over the white George Segal statues.
"That was fun. Dana, where you from?"
"Was born in Ohio. I've got some real estate on Fire
    Island.
Holidays I crew at Radio City. Just sailed over from
    Fort Lauderdale a few days ago. What do you
    do?"
"I do all kinds of things, Dana."

Dana understands.

Twilight reveals early constellations on Titania's arm
    veins.

They talk and then:

"Titania, I'm having dinner with some friends, have
    to go, pleasure to meet you. Maybe we can hang
    some other time."

"Sure, I'd love that."

Goodbye kisses in the air to avoid spoiling makeup.

Titania returns to The Monster.

A drag queen sings *Les Miserables'* "I Dreamed a
    Dream."

Titania orders another beer and goes back to dance.

Titania Discovers Cherry Grove

"Hi, Titania, I'm China.
I have a place in Cherry Grove.
It's a ferry away from Sayville, Long Island
after you take the LIRR from
Penn Station.
Been visiting paradise for decades now."
China: platinum wig.
Tight animal print dress.
Pink high heels.
Cool makeup.
Girl, you are beautiful.

National seashore protected beach.
Serene, like a sheet of blue.
Surrounded by dunes sprinkled
with beach grass.
"You can even go naked
on the shore.
I'll be going this weekend.
Come with me?"

After the crowded but friendly
ride—no need to stay quiet here!—
they take a photo
under the "Welcome to Cherry Grove" sign.

China opens her closet,
full of wigs,

China

shoes,
dresses,
feather boas,
and
headdresses.
A vanity with a
beveled oval mirror.
Makeup and jewelry.

After having a few drinks
and giggling through
the process,
they create magic.
China brings out the Mary Ann
in Titania
and becomes Ginger.

Sequined dress,
beauty mark on her face.

Titania is blown away
by all the gay people,
trans people, even hetero
getting happily drunk.
But mostly by all the compliments
on her costume.
And the way "girl" falls so naturally
from their lips
as they follow her
with their eyes.
The Ice Palace itself.
"You're adorable"
seems to echo from its gaudy
but loving walls.

And yes, they win.
She knew but didn't know it.

As Titania and China claim the stage,
first prize winners,
Titania thinks to herself,
"I belong here."

The DJ blasts
Gilligan's Island theme song.

THE SECOND PANDEMIC

In a city hospital hall,
nurses and doctors
are overworked,
running back and forth
between loud beeping ventilators.
Titania lies on a stretcher in the hall
waiting for a bed.
It's been hours since she was found
on the floor of the emergency room.
The fluid in her lungs starts to
silence her fading beat.
From the crowds,
while gasping for air,
she sees Mom.
Titania clutches her rosary,
the one she remembers her mom
wearing forever,
now around Titania's neck.
"Mom, what are you doing here?"
No answer.
Titania's dusky gray life takes over her skin.
The crucifix sheds Titania's last grip on life.
Among strangers,
forgotten by god,
she stops breathing.
Covid, her second pandemic,
claims another Jane Doe.

Months after:

Candles.
Piece of cardboard with a picture and date:
1961–2021.
Circle of roses, ribbons
with a "T" inside
on the Christopher Street corner
near Boots and Saddle,
now gone.
"To Our Titania. In our hearts always."

REMEMBERING

I remember
you,
girl,
hiding
behind Francisco's
smile.
Painting rainbows
with chalk
on the sidewalks
of the Lower East Side.
I am there
the first
time
you try on
one of mom's
dresses.
And the
mirror
unveils
Titania.
Full blown
with
a touch
of
"blood rose"
(mom's lipstick),
sparkly
sky
eye

shadow.
Eyeliner
like Cleopatra.
Evangeline
splash
from
the bottle
sitting on
the vanity
with the
round mirror
grandma
left behind.
Titania
is alone
in mom's
bedroom.
Only
a picture
of
St. Francis of Assisi
tacked to
the wall
and I
watch her
being born.

What a pleasure
to walk New York City
in your high heels
we buy together

from a thrift store
on
14th Street.
Smiling
to admirers,
giving the
middle finger
to envious haters.
I find myself
missing
your getting ready
to visit
The Village
and celebrating
your skills
skating in Central Park.
Within me
I still can feel
Ricardo's
lust
which
wakes up
a thousand times
the need for
more than
johns
and their
money
to get
the fix.
Titania,

the interrupted
song of
your pulse
lives
forever
on my
keyboard.

   Fire Island and Their Sister

ABOUT PEARLSONG PRESS

Pearlsong Press is an independent publishing company dedicated to providing books and resources that entertain while expanding perspectives on the self and the world. The company was founded by psychologist Peggy Elam, Ph.D.

FICTION

If We Were Snowflakes—YA novel by Barbara D'Souza

Heretics: A Love Story & *The Singing of Swans*—novels about the divine feminine by Mary Saracino

Judith & *Under the Pomegranate Tree*—historical novels by Leslie Moïse

Fatropolis—paranormal adventure by Tracey L. Thompson

The Falstaff Vampire Files, Bride of the Living Dead, Larger Than Death, Large Target, At Large & *A Ton of Trouble*—paranormal adventure, romantic comedy & Josephine Fuller mysteries by Lynne Murray

The Season of Lost Children—a novel by Karen Blomain

Fallen Embers & *Blowing Embers*—Books 1 & 2 of The Embers Series, paranormal romance by Lauri J Owen

The Program & *The Fat Lady Sings*—suspense & YA novels by Charlie Lovett

Syd Arthur—a novel by Ellen Frankel

Measure By Measure—a romantic romp with the fabulously fat by Rebecca Fox & William Sherman

FatLand & *FatLand: The Early Days*—Books 1 & 2 of The FatLand Trilogy by Frannie Zellman

ROMANCE NOVELS & SHORT STORIES FEATURING BIG BEAUTIFUL HEROINES

by Pat Ballard, the Queen of Rubenesque Romances:
Once Upon Another Time | *Adam & Evelyn* | *ASAP Nanny*
Dangerous Love | *The Best Man* | *Abigail's Revenge*

Dangerous Curves Ahead: Short Stories | *Wanted: One Groom*
Nobody's Perfect | *His Brother's Child* | *A Worthy Heir*
by Rebecca Brock—*The Giving Season*
& by Judy Bagshaw—*Kiss Me, Nate!* & *At Long Last, Love*

NONFICTION

Flying On Invisible Wings & *Poems of Reckoning and Hope*—
poetry by Félix Garmendía
Fat Poets Speak: Voices of the Fat Poets' Society, Fat Poets
Speak 2: Living and Loving Fatly, & *Fat Poets Speak 3:*
FatDance Flying—Frannie Zellman, Ed.
Other Nations: An Animal Journal—poetry by Maria Famà
Soul Mothers' Wisdom: Seven Insights for the Single Mother
by Bette J. Freedson
Acceptable Prejudice? Fat, Rhetoric & Social Justice & *Talking*
Fat: Health vs. Persuasion in the War on Our Bodies
by Lonie McMichael, Ph.D.
Hiking the Pack Line: Moving from Grief to a Joyful Life
by Bonnie Shapbell
A Life Interrupted: Living with Brain Injury—poetry
by Louise Mathewson
ExtraOrdinary: An End of Life Story Without End—memoir
by Michele Tamaren & Michael Wittner
Love is the Thread: A Knitting Friendship
by Leslie Moïse, Ph.D.
10 Steps to Loving Your Body by Pat Ballard
Beyond Measure: A Memoir About Short Stature & Inner
Growth by Ellen Frankel
Taking Up Space by Pattie Thomas, Ph.D.
with Carl Wilkerson, M.B.A.
Off Kilter—a memoir by Linda C. Wisniewski
Unconventional Means: The Dream Down Under—
a spiritual travelogue by Anne Richardson Williams
Splendid Seniors: Great Lives, Great Deeds—inspirational
biographies by Jack Adler